Love Is a Side Effect of Life

Andy Lee

ISBN 978-1-9992073-0-4 (chapbook)
ISBN 978-1-9992073-1-1 (ebook)

Photos and design by Andy Lee

Published by Casa del Alma

For Umma

Astral Travel

I dissolve deep in your dimension,
purple planes, echoes perpetual
from plaintive mechanical jackals.

Lost, scattered to dust
under a sanguine sun. Sea knows
your secrets; I know your ghost.

I ascend from your depths, reformed
from ether to fibre: a chariot piercing
the pale horizon, a nameless soul reborn.

Reverie

limbs reaching to infinity, encompassing
fauna, flora, first errors, fatal kisses,
I rise toward light
soar through cobalt corridors
plunge into an upright ocean suspended
between colossal capitalist columns
inverse freefall
revolución coursing across synapses
tumbling into the soft cosmos
before plummeting back
to the cold, flat earth.

Never Leave a Burning Child Unattended

Precocious wings flutter. Futile. Shuttered dream
factory. Shed the husk of recycled daylight.

Prefab life. Feeling destructed. Lost among the dollar
stores and crack whores of Cabbagetown.

Prehistoric punchline. Your mouth, a kingdom. I want
to drown in your amniotic ocean.

Pretty girl, my Sausalito paramour. Forty, no
passport, never seen New York.

Pretend we're still innocent. Let's melt supernovas
on our tongues and wait for the sun to die.

Bumbling Through Love

Burnt by Tinder, I tumble
down the Bumble funnel,
swiped and winnowed by
nubiles narcissists widows
casualties of worn love
genetic runners-up
in a vast matchmaker apparatus
chock-full of duck faces trout pouts
cock pics fuckfaces loudmouths
tan lines delineating bare flesh
hierarchy of abdominals chests
group shots clutter, hide blurred lives
ponytail looped through blue ball cap
a ruse for male gaze
I attempt to exit unscathed
but something inside,
unsaid, has changed.

Love Is a Side Effect of Life

In the end, it's beauty that kills
you. I knew that once.

I follow your vagabond heart to the desert
only to find you
circling black skies above the Pacific.

Your ways held in ancient cipher,
lost in the heads of dead sages.

I detect latent danger in clouds,
every breeze an apparition.

Clutching faded emblems
I wait for you,
watch the reverse birth of Osiris.

In the morning I awake alone,
bleeding from your kiss.

Loving You Is a Cloisterfuck

Not long ago, you and I were
everyone's envy but now we're
dancing in circles with our other lovers'
other lovers, always thirsting
for next flesh, a fresh heart,
deplorable, explorable,
unknowable. A failed Hail Mary,
loving you is a cloisterfuck.

You redact me for the last time.
Heatseeker still locked on my heart.
I trawl galaxies but your secret name
evades. You and I, once cognates,
now lost in semantic gaps
dead tongues eddying through
his story, my present, your dust
brushing the stars from below.

From Love's Gutter

From love's gutter
watching the world march by
paired up, moved on
I, meanwhile, neither dad nor dyad
nor graciously dead.

Dropped out of the race
my name phases away
time reduces us all
eschewing new circles
for next nostalgia.

A Country Song

We didn't know his father –
liquored-up at that party –
when he came, it was a country song:
"I'm a little bit drunk,
you're a little bit high"

a cluster of stars, a
million-dollar mistake;
a buffer between
your heart and
his charisma.

Desert Poem

Sandstorms can cause caravans to lose their way.
Heavenly lies cut off the corridor, forked
around the oasis two millennia ago.

Resisting invasions, he dispatched claims
to sovereignty, the new frontier
completely under control.

Take me along a line that follows the charred
edge of the evening sun hanging low in a red-gray sky,
burning blackened village women, blowing dust:

The hottest, lowest place.

Exit Wound

you used to want me. Now
we're forty-five, friends,
an example of dying.

a crooked picture hanging for no one
   a life without any ties
      – satisfied?

I'm an illusion, a scarlet speck
at the back of your throat:
vomit; I'm gone.

Hunter

Hunter for parts untouched
devoid of deceit, deep in the void we meet
swapping dagger wounds under a strawberry moon.

I chase your memory through fields of lavender
feel the first kiss of rain like teenage
lips on teenage lips.

One hand on your thigh
the other clutching a moist bomb,
ready to blow.

Conch

Exhumed from Exuma
bearded speedboat stowaway
coast clear on hotel bathroom counter
an alien appears
blinking bulbous
accusatory eyes

prisoner in paper bag
to the lobby where a sultry band
covers Frank Ocean as dark
waves tumble outside

where headland strives for moonlight
creature raised in a fist
hurled back to habitat
seeking a current home
pulled by forces unseen
like the hands of man.

Sea Dream

I see you in Bondi blue
from a distant coastal roadway:
a solar goldburst riding liquid land,
underswells immune to your ephemeral dance.

Aquarian accomplice born in a cerulean sphere
out there, one with the ocean. From here I watch, wait
like a dry shore pining for
your tidal embrace.

Death in the Evening

Four murders in two hours
and no one cried foul,
least of all the gringo bro
in Ray-Bans and white polo
swilling beer, dumping
sunflower husks onto the stone floor of
Las Ventas like it was Wrigley Field.
"We've gotten too soft," he snarled
at his beta buddy, a nodding automaton.
"Trump oughta bring this to the U.S."
As we watched exalted conspirators loose
blood from broken bulls, sullying the dirt floor
like thousands of innocents before, my horror
grew in proportion to his hard-on for carnage.
After the fourth coup de grâce, I sidestepped
from the crime scene, trailed by a wary gaze
as I scrambled back to the sultry arteries of Madrid.

The Periphery of Memory

As time shears your mind away
you hug me like it's been months
instead of days, days that are dissolving
for you. Lately you embrace me
like you did when I was young,
a feeling on the periphery of memory,
before I grew and you stopped.

If there's light in your darkness,
a purpose to your curse, perhaps
your loss is my bliss. For as you slip
toward our creator, we are
sliding back to love.

Seeker

I trace your name in stars
still seek you in the dark
sling signals across
a city asleep
rendezvous in dreams
waltzing in alpha waves
but in nothing we wake

Tender Trap

headlong plunge into
your tender trap

I come in pieces
against your hard surfaces

pre-demented,
ready to tango

Generation Hexed

we are a generation hexed
born bored, addicted to next
connected and severed like
never before by high-tech

manic animals craving a glib fix
too busy broadcasting personas to
personas to fathom the aftertaste
of silence, or a lifetime of waste

Carbon Copy

Your third life starts the split second you die
from a vaccination gone awry. Consolation:
consciousness restored from a lifetime of metadata
hoarded on Google servers. Virtual no more,
a superhuman subroutine emerges from
primordial digital soup, an avatar so flawless
your lover and mother barely notice
the quiet fleck of death gleaming somewhere
just beyond pale blue eyes.

Poetry Shall Persist

Who dares write poetry anymore?
Only lovers and fools.
A gasping art reviled by modern man
Revived during times of turmoil.

When everything has been said

Poetry shall persist.
When every human nuance has been quantized
Poets will still toil with the inscrutable,
To make the ineffable indelible.

Final Call

When my ashes dance again with the dust of all existence
exhume and resurrect my words so I live infinite
in future minds, an unbroken human helix
carrying code through time intertwixt.

Scatter my seeds to soporific skies
let them chute confetti cargo,
fertile fallout for thirsty earth
yawning at dawn.

Standard Deviation

Now that the oxytocin has oxidized and I've fallen
from your favourites list, I don't feel bad that
you don't invite me for bowling, hot dogs
and Molson Ex on Monday night.

Early frost warning ignored. Addicted to
abuse, delicious relapse. In constant
fear of your pendulum's vengeance.
Bitter granite enveloped in petals.

A naked flame wandering the cold
shores of a wasteland ruled by
reptilian heritage. Still a willing
prisoner in your mechanical hell.

I'm a tangerine you peel
my skin, pierce my flesh, suck
my juices dry, chew through
sinew, spit used fibres.

Found a deity in the abyss. You
linger on my lips. Your dead
skin cells cloud my horizon. Red
light at dawn sets false hope in motion.

You cultivate joy for one, a sequestered
expert in self-sabotage. Unstable radon
daughter. Fun now, barren later. Stares
shared like bacteria between strangers.

Absent from your agenda, a seasonal
affect sloughed off like Winnipeg wellies
caked with salt and dirt and black grime.
Excised from summer plans and life dreams.

Deflated elation. Feline gaze for foreigners.
In a vision she's breastfeeding a blue whale.
It ends here; no friends here. I'm leaving
the bright lights now — don't follow me.

Years later, we meet in an east-end coffee shop:
grey hair and brittle skin, rubbing imprints
from sapphire shards and straining to recall
the harmonies of a long-forgotten song.

Acknowledgments

Thank you to Robert Priest for feedback, encouragement
and inspiration.

Thanks to Mike Drach for spot-on on-the-spot proofing.

The author gratefully acknowledges C*SARN and the
Toronto Arts Council for supporting the creation of
these poems.

Merci beaucoup to the editors of *Vallum* magazine,
in which "Carbon Copy" originally appeared.

About the Author

Andy Lee (@realandylee) is an award-winning writer, poet, lyricist, musician and member of the Writers Guild of Canada. He writes stories for adults and children, for screen and print. Andy has incanted his poems at the International Festival of Authors, the Nuyorican Poets Café in New York City, down under in Australia and on the playa of the Black Rock Desert, among other places. His poetry has appeared in *Vallum* magazine and was shortlisted for their 2017 Chapbook Award.

www.ingramcontent.com/pod-product-compliance
Lightning Source LLC
Chambersburg PA
CBHW051511050726
47594CB00010B/4059